Life in a Medieval Monastery

Marc Cels

 Crabtree Publishing Company

www.crabtreebooks.com

Crabtree Publishing Company

www.crabtreebooks.com

Coordinating editor: Ellen Rodger

Project editor: Carrie Gleason

Editor: Rachel Eagen

Designer and production coordinator: Rosie Gowsell

Scanning technician: Arlene Arch-Wilson

Art director: Rob MacGregor

Project development, editing, photo editing, and layout:
First Folio Resource Group, Inc.: Tom Dart, Debbie Smith, Anikó Szocs

Proofreading: Lynne Elliott

Photo research: Maria DeCambra

Consultant: Isabelle Cochelin, University of Toronto

Photographs: Art Archive/Bibliothèque Municipale Valenciennes/Dagli Orti: p. 7; Art Archive/Bodleian Library Oxford/Ashmole 1462 folio 31r: p. 8 (right); Art Archive/British Library: p. 8 (left); Art Archive/Dagli Orti: p. 29 (top); Art Archive/Klosterneuburg Monastery Austria/Dagli Orti: p. 29 (bottom); Art Archive/Museo de Arte Antiga Lisbon/Dagli Orti: p. 19; Art Archive/Real biblioteca de lo Escorial/Dagli Orti: p. 18; Art Resource, NY: p. 23 (top left); British Library/Add. 74236 p. 524: p. 11 (left); British Library/Cotton Nero D. VII f.27: p. 13 (left); British Library/Harley 4425 f.11: p. 16 (right); British Library/Royal 16 G. VI f.368v: p. 9 (top); British Library/Royal 20 D. VI f.213v: p. 9 (bottom); British Library/Topham-HIP/The Image Works: p. 22; British Library/Yates Thompson 11 f.6v: p. 12; Jean Marc Charles/Corbis Sygma/Magma: p. 31 (bottom right); Church of St. Quiriace, Provins, France, Lauros/Giraudon/Bridgeman Art Library: p. 6 (bottom); Gianni Dagli Orti/Corbis/Magma: p. 24 (right); Giraudon/Art Resource, NY: title page, p. 24 (left); Hanan Isachar/Corbis/Magma: p. 31 (top right); Erich Lessing/Art Resource, NY: p. 4, p. 6 (top), p. 13 (right), p. 16 (left), Museum of Yaroslavl, Russia/Bridgeman Art Library: p. 25 (center right); National Library, St. Petersburg, Russia/Bridgeman Art Library: p. 17 (right); Pierpont Morgan Library/Art Resource, NY: p. 10 (top), p. 11 (right); Fulvio Roiter/Corbis/Magma: p. 30 (right); Royal Asiatic Society, London/Bridgeman Art Library: p. 23 (center right); Scala/Art Resource, NY: cover, p. 17 (left), p. 21 (right), p. 25 (bottom left); Snark/Art Resource, NY: p. 23 (bottom left); Arthur Thévenart/Corbis/Magma: p. 28; Sandro Vannini/Corbis/Magma: p. 31 (center left); C. Walker/Topham/The Image Works: p. 25 (top left); Julia Waterlow, Eye Ubiquitous/Corbis/Magma: p. 30 (left)

Map: Samara Parent, Margaret Amy Reaich

Illustrations: Jeff Crosby: pp. 26–27; Katherine Kantor: flags, title page (border), copyright page (bottom); Margaret Amy Reiach: borders, gold boxes, title page (illuminated letter), copyright page (top), contents page (background), pp. 4-5 (timeline), p. 5 (pyramid), p. 21 (top), p. 32 (all)

Cover: Monks and nuns lived in communities called monasteries. They studied the Rule of their monastery to learn how to live a religious life through work, study, and prayer.

Title page: Monks and nuns spent much of their day singing prayers and songs from the Bible in their monastery's church.

Crabtree Publishing Company

www.crabtreebooks.com   1-800-387-7650

Cataloging-in-Publication Data
Cels, Marc.
   Life in a medieval monastery : the medieval world / written by Marc Cels.
   p. cm.
   Includes index.
   ISBN 0-7787-1352-0 (rlb) -- ISBN 0-7787-1384-9 (pbk.)
   1. Monasticism and religious orders--History--Middle Ages, 600-1500--Juvenile literature. 2. Monastic and religious life--History--Middle Ages, 600-1500--Juvenile literature.
   I. Title.
   BX2470.C35 2004
   271'.009'02--dc22
                                                    2004013059
                                                          LC

Published in the United States
PMB 16A
350 Fifth Ave.
Suite 3308
New York, NY
10118

Published in Canada
616 Welland Ave.,
St. Catharines,
Ontario, Canada
L2M 5V6

Published in the United Kingdom
73 Lime Walk
Headington
Oxford
0X3 7AD
United Kingdom

Published in Australia
386 Mt. Alexander Rd.,
Ascot Vale (Melbourne)
V1C 3032

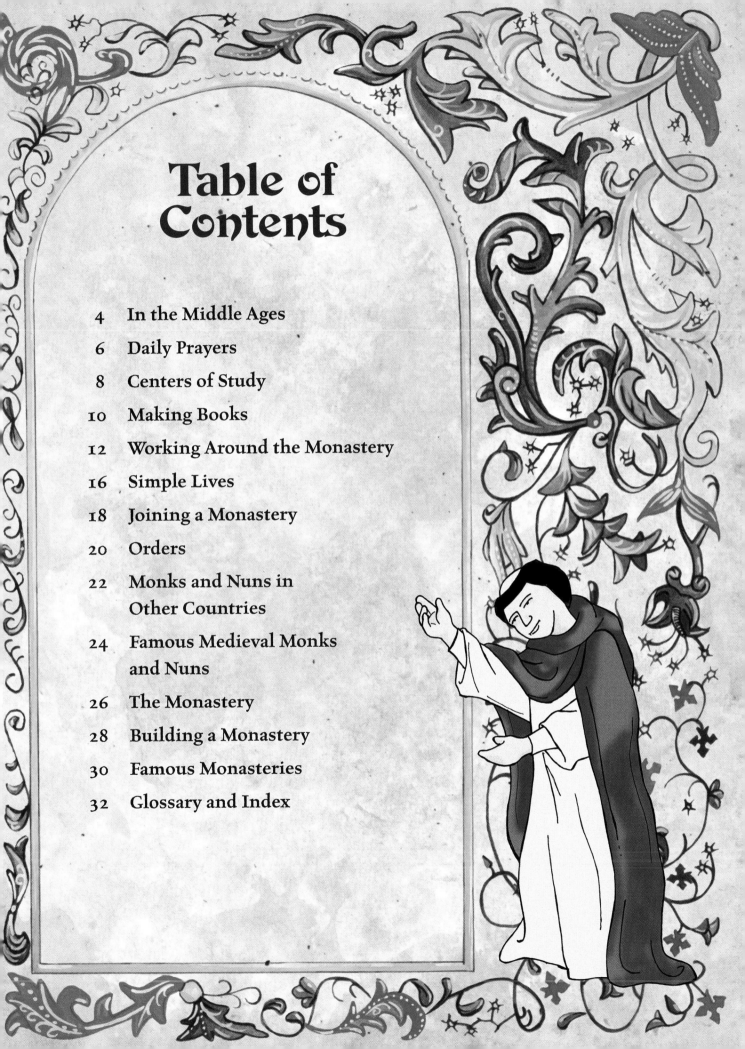

Table of Contents

In the Middle Ages

The period from about 500 A.D. to 1500 A.D. is called the Middle Ages, or the medieval period, of western Europe. Medieval Europe was divided into many kingdoms and territories ruled by lords, such as kings and nobles, who often went to war against each other for more honor, land, and wealth.

During the Middle Ages, most people were peasants who farmed their lords' lands. Others settled in towns where they worked as **merchants** or **tradespeople**. Some men and women led religious lives as priests, monks, or nuns.

Medieval Religion

In the Middle Ages, most people in western Europe were Christians. Christians believe in one God and follow the teachings of Jesus Christ, who they believe is God's son. Religion was an important part of everyday life. Medieval Christians believed that if they led good lives, they would be rewarded in **Heaven** after they died. Every Sunday, they went to church for a religious service called Mass, and they celebrated Christian holy days throughout the year.

▲ *Monks and nuns lived in communities called monasteries. Many monasteries were built of stone by tradespeople known as masons.*

Christianity becomes the main religion in Europe
300s

St. Benedict of Nursia, in Italy, writes the Benedictine Rule for monks
480–547

Most Catholic monks and nuns follow the Benedictine Rule
800s

Monastery of Cluny, in France, is founded
910

Order of Cistercian monks founded in France
1098

430
St. Patrick brings Christianity to Ireland

552
Monks bring Buddhism to Japan

800–950
Non-Christians from outside Europe destroy many monasteries

1054
Split between Roman Catholic and Eastern Orthodox Church

▲ *During the Middle Ages, the Christians of western Europe were mostly Roman Catholic, led by the Pope (yellow). In eastern Europe, most people belonged to a different branch of Christianity, the Eastern Orthodox Church (green). The two branches of Christianity had different customs, but both had monks and nuns. People in parts of Spain, Africa, and the Middle East were Muslim (orange).*

Monks and Nuns

Some very religious men, called monks, and women, called nuns, devoted their lives to God. They gave up their personal belongings and families to live stricter lives than most other Christians. Monks and nuns lived separately in communities called monasteries. Communities of nuns are also known as convents. They spent their time praying, studying religious books such as the Bible, and working inside the monasteries. They also gave charity, in the form of money and help, to those in need. They cared for the sick and housed travelers.

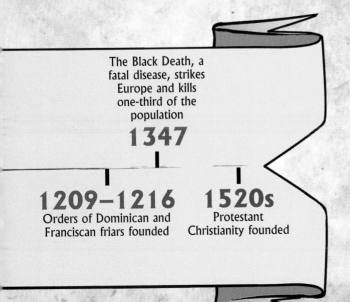

The Black Death, a fatal disease, strikes Europe and kills one-third of the population
1347

1209–1216
Orders of Dominican and Franciscan friars founded

1520s
Protestant Christianity founded

▲ *Kings and powerful nobles gave large areas of land, called manors, to monasteries, Church leaders, and less important nobles.*

Daily Prayers

Between twelve and two hundred monks or nuns usually lived in a monastery. They lived by a set of instructions, called a Rule, that guided everything they did for every hour of the day. The most important activity was prayer. Monks and nuns prayed to honor and thank God, to ask forgiveness for their sins and the sins of others, and to request help in protecting the people and crops of the country.

Members of monasteries prayed in the church ten times each day. There were eight scheduled prayer services, called the Divine Office, at which monks or nuns listened to religious readings in **Latin** and sang prayers and poems from the Bible. The Bible is a collection of holy writings that tell Christians how to live in a way that will please God.

▲ *Nuns counted their prayers using strings of beads called rosaries.*

Twice a day, monks and nuns attended Mass. At Mass, a priest chanted prayers that recalled the last supper Jesus ate with his closest followers the night before he was crucified, or put to death on a cross. The priest also blessed holy wine and bread, called Communion. Christians believe that the wine represents Jesus' blood and the bread represents his body. The monks or nuns occasionally received Communion by sharing the bread and wine, after confessing their sins to a priest and obtaining forgiveness.

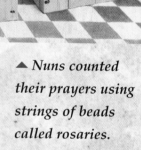

▶ *During Mass, the wine for Communion was placed in a cup called a chalice, and the bread was placed on a dish called a paten.*

The Schedule in a Benedictine Monastery

From the 1100s onward, monks and nuns divided themselves into different groups, or orders. Most belonged to the Benedictine Order and followed the Rule written by Saint Benedict, who lived from 480 to 550. Benedictines, like other monks and nuns, followed a regular schedule, or *horarium*, of prayer, private reading, work around the monastery, and rest. The schedule changed with the seasons. In the summer, when the days were longer, monks and nuns ate two meals and had a nap during the day. In the winter, when days were shorter, they ate only one meal, had a drink break, and went to bed early.

▶ *Saint Benedict shown giving his set of Rules to monks and nuns. The saint is shown as larger to show his importance.*

A Monk's Winter *Horarium*

Time	Activity
3:00 a.m.	Matins: the first prayer service of the day
5:00 a.m.	Reading
6:00 a.m.	Lauds: a short prayer service at dawn; Prime: another short prayer service
7:30 a.m.	Reading
8:00 a.m.	Wash and change; Terce: a short prayer service; short Mass; Chapter meeting, during which a chapter was read from the Rule of St. Benedict.
9:45 a.m.	Work
12:00 p.m.	Sext: a short prayer service; longer Mass
1:20 p.m.	None: a short prayer service, from which the word "noon" derives
2:00 p.m.	Dinner
2:45 p.m.	Work
4:15 p.m.	Vespers: a longer prayer service that included prayers for the dead; Drink break
6:00 p.m.	Collatio: the monks listened to a reading or lecture
6:15 p.m.	Compline: a short prayer service
6:30 p.m.	Bedtime

Centers of Study

Medieval monasteries were centers of learning. Monks and nuns read books about religion, especially the Bible, stories about the lives of saints, and writings that explained how to be better Christians. They learned how to sing the Divine Office and teach religion to other Christians.

Monks and nuns studied other subjects too, believing that they could learn more about God by studying everything in the universe that God created. They read lapidaries, which are books about rocks and gems; herbals, which are books about plants; and bestiaries, which are books about animals. They also studied books of **philosophy**, science, medicine, history, and poetry that were written by ancient Greeks and Romans. Some monks and nuns also wrote their own poetry, plays, and history books.

▲ Monks and nuns studied books about plants so they could learn about God's creations and how to make medicines to help the sick.

◀ Bede the Venerable (672–735) was a monk who became one of the most famous medieval writers. He wrote a history of how the English people became Christians, as well as books about the lives of saints, explanations of the Bible, and books about science.

Giving Advice

Until 1100, monks and nuns were the most educated people in medieval Europe. Most other people could not afford to buy books and did not know how to read and write. Kings and Church leaders often hired educated monks to give them advice on how to manage and rule their lands.

▶ *Some monasteries ran schools where the children of nobles were taught Latin, basic mathematics, and religion.*

Missionaries

At the beginning of the Middle Ages, monks and nuns from southern Europe spread the lessons of Jesus Christ to northern Europe. They were called missionaries. At the time, people in northern Europe worshiped many gods and spirits in nature. The missionaries destroyed **temples** built to honor these gods and constructed monasteries and churches in their place. They also brought education, books, writing, and new forms of art to the northern lands.

It took hundreds of years for Christianity to become the religion of most Europeans. Some traditional customs and holidays continued to be observed, or became part of the Christian calendar. Many missionary monks became famous saints, such as Saint Patrick (385–451), who brought Christianity to the Irish, and Saint Boniface (680–754), who brought Christianity to Germany.

▲ *Patrick spent many years in Ireland as a British slave. After he escaped and became a monk, he had dreams in which God told him to return to Ireland as a missionary.*

Making Books

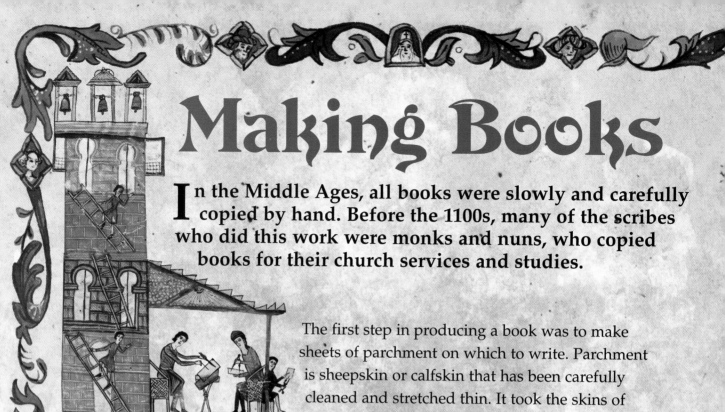

In the Middle Ages, all books were slowly and carefully copied by hand. Before the 1100s, many of the scribes who did this work were monks and nuns, who copied books for their church services and studies.

▲ *Scribes worked in a room called a scriptorium, which had large windows that let in sunlight.*

The first step in producing a book was to make sheets of parchment on which to write. Parchment is sheepskin or calfskin that has been carefully cleaned and stretched thin. It took the skins of 200 sheep to make a book as large as the Bible.

A team of scribes often shared the work of copying and decorating a manuscript, or medieval book. Scribes were trained to use the same style of writing so that it was difficult to tell one monk's writing from another's. They used special tools to do their work.

▼ *Scribes dipped their pens in ink placed in little pots or animal horns called inkwells. The ink was made by mixing soot, which is the powder left behind after wood is burned, with thickeners, such as tree sap.*

▲ *Scribes used a pointed metal tool called a stylus to draw lines and margins on the page so they knew where to write.*

▲ *Pens were made from dried reeds or large bird feathers called quills. The ends of pens were sharpened to points with pen knives.*

Manuscript Masterpieces

Scribes honored God and the saints by decorating religious books with colorful illustrations and borders. Initial, or first, letters were often filled in with tiny drawings or designs to help readers find the beginning of chapters. To make these illustrations, scribes used colored inks, paints made from ground **pigments** mixed with egg yolk, and very thin pieces of gold that were glued to the page. Books decorated with gold were called illuminated manuscripts because of the way they glowed.

▲ The covers of books containing prayers and Bible readings were sometimes decorated with silver, gold, and gemstones. This German prayer book, called the Berthold Missal, includes little sculptures and relics of saints. It was displayed on the altar of a monastery's church.

◀ The Sherbourne Missal contains prayers said by monks during Mass every day of the year. Small paintings on this page illustrate the life of Mary, the mother of Jesus Christ, and show monks singing to her.

Working Around the Monastery

The superior, or head, of a monastery of monks was called an abbot, and the head of a community of nuns was called an abbess. Superiors kept order in the monastery. They led daily Chapter meetings, at which they taught monks and nuns how to serve God, praised members who had done their work well, and punished those who had broken the monastery's Rule. They also led discussions about monastery business, such as which new members to admit to the monastery.

Many abbots and abbesses also ruled land that they had been given by kings and other nobles. They collected taxes, rents, and fines from the people who lived on their land, judged cases in court, and provided knights to their lords.

▲ *Priests or abbots from other monasteries often supervised abbesses. Priests also performed Mass for communities of nuns, since women were not allowed to do so. The abbess, prioress, and cellaress still took part in the church service, along with nuns whose responsibilities included ringing church bells and carrying prayer books.*

Prior and Prioress

The second in command was the prior or prioress. While the abbot or abbess was busy ruling the land, the prior or prioress supervised members of the monastery. In large monasteries, priors or prioresses were sometimes assisted by subpriors or subprioresses. Some monasteries, called priories, did not have abbots or abbesses. They were ruled by priors or prioresses who reported to abbots of other monasteries.

▼ *Abbots and abbesses carried curved shepherds' staffs as symbols of their leadership. Abbots sometimes also wore pointed hats called miters.*

Farming

Monasteries had fields where crops such as wheat, rye, and oats were grown for food, and land where animals such as cows, pigs, and sheep grazed. These animals were raised for their milk, meat, and wool. Some farmwork was done by monks or nuns, but many monasteries had servants so that monks or nuns could devote more time to prayer. Beginning in the 1100s, some orders had lay brothers or lay sisters who did the physical work. These were peasants who took the vows of monks or nuns, but did not know how to read, sing the Divine Office, or perform Mass. They lived apart from the others, in separate quarters within the monastery.

▲ *In the Middle Ages, most farmwork was done by hand. Monks harvested their fields of grain in the autumn using curved knives called sickles, and they bundled the stalks into sheaves.*

Special Responsibilities

The superior gave some monks or nuns special responsibilities around the monastery. Cellarers or cellaresses made sure that monasteries had enough food, clothing, and shelter for their members. They supervised servants and hired other workers to repair buildings and tools. They also brought in food from nearby towns and collected rents from peasants who lived on land owned by the monastery. The cellarer delegated many jobs to assistants.

◄ The kitchener was in charge of preparing food in the monastery kitchen.

▶ The refectorer made sure the refectory, or dining area, was prepared and cleaned for each meal.

▶ The chamberlain gave monks and nuns clothing, shoes, towels, and sheets.

▼ The precentor or precentoress directed the monastery choir during the Divine Office. Occasionally, he or she supervised all the writing and bookmaking in the monastery, served as the librarian, and helped monks or nuns who were studying.

▶ The novice–master or novice–mistress supervised the education of novices, who were people learning how to be monks or nuns.

◀ The sacristan was in charge of decorating, cleaning, and repairing the monastery's church. The sacristan also provided supplies for Mass, including candles, sacred dishes, and prayer books.

▶ The hosteller or guestmaster provided shelter for guests and travelers, such as Church leaders or nobles with their servants and attendants.

▼ The infirmarian took care of sick and injured monks and nuns, as well as sick villagers and townspeople who arrived at the monastery asking for help. Medicines were made from the roots, leaves, or seeds of plants grown in the garden.

◀ The almoner handed out leftover food, grain, and used clothing to those in need.

Simple Lives

Monks and nuns led simple lives according to the monastery's Rule. The Rule told them not only when to pray, work, and study, but also how and when to eat, dress, cut their hair, wash, and talk.

Monks and nuns spent most of their days in silence to encourage thought and prayer. They sang and read aloud during church services and were permitted to talk to each other, if necessary, while at work, in the **cloister**, or in rooms called parlors, where quiet speaking was allowed. In most monasteries, a simple sign language was used to communicate during the long hours of silence. Some orders of monks and nuns kept strict silence at all times, except while praying.

Clothing

Monks and nuns wore long, woolen gowns called habits. They also cut their hair in ways that set them apart from other people.

- Monks shaved the tops and bottoms of their heads. This type of haircut was called a tonsure.
- Nuns kept their hair short. They covered their heads and necks with wimples and loose veils. Wimples were long pieces of cloth wrapped around the head.
- Monks sometimes wore a hood called a cowl.
- Monks and nuns wore habits made of wool dyed black, brown, gray, or white. Some wore belts called cinctures.
- Nuns and monks wore capes outdoors in cool weather.

▲ In the refectory, the monastery community ate meals together in silence and listened as a monk or nun read stories from books about saints.

Meals

Meals were served in the refectory. There was only one meal a day during the winter, but two meals were served during the longer days of summer. Meals were supposed to consist of small amounts of simple foods, such as bread, boiled vegetables, nuts, fruits, cheese, fish, and some wine or beer, but monks and nuns were often allowed to eat finer foods, including poultry. On Christmas, Easter, and other holy days, the community feasted on extra dishes of eggs and fish. On fast days, which came before holy days, monks and nuns ate little or no food. The longest fast was Lent, the period of 40 days before Easter.

Hygiene

In the cloister was a fountain called a lavatorium, where members of the monastery washed their hands and faces before entering the church or refectory. Monks and nuns usually washed their feet only once a week. Bathing was less frequent, usually three or four times a year in tubs that the chamberlain filled with water.

Time to Sleep

Members of monasteries slept in large rooms called dormitories, on beds with straw mattresses and wool blankets. Monks and nuns slept in their habits to protect their **modesty** and keep them warm in the unheated dormitories. They also wore their slippers to bed so that they were ready for the first prayer service in the very early hours of the morning. By the end of the Middle Ages, dormitories were divided into private cells, in which monks or nuns slept and studied alone.

▼ When a monk or nun died, a priest performed the funeral service as the body was buried in the monastery's cemetery. The rest of the community prayed that the dead person's soul would go to Heaven.

Joining a Monastery

Some people joined monasteries because they felt called by God. Others joined to get a good education and become scholars or even abbots or abbesses. Some women became nuns because they did not want to marry. Men and women who wished to join a monastery were expected to donate money, land, or other gifts, so many monks and nuns came from wealthier families who could afford to do so.

Oblates

During the early Middle Ages, parents gave children as young as seven years old to monasteries. They hoped that their children's prayers would help the family, and that their children would be well-cared for, educated, and have good careers. These children became child monks or nuns known as oblates.

Older monks or nuns taught oblates Latin and how to sing. Caregivers called Masters of Children watched over the oblates and helped them learn the rules and routines of the monastery. Oblates were not supposed to laugh, and only some monasteries allowed them to play, usually once a week or once a month. Oblates did have some special privileges. For example, bowls of hot coals were placed beside them in the refectory to keep them warm. After the age of fifteen, oblates left the care of the Masters of Children and followed all the rules of the adult monks and nuns.

▲ *In this illustration, an angel accepts a family's gift to the monastery (top). The family is bringing their child to live as an oblate (middle). The oblate is led into the monastery, then he is given a monk's robe (bottom).*

Waiting to Join

By the 1100s, many monasteries stopped accepting oblates. Abbots and abbesses thought that children in monasteries distracted monks and nuns who needed quiet to focus on religious practices. They also thought that children should wait until they were teenagers to join the monastery, when they were old enough to understand their decision and agree to follow the Rule.

Novices

If teenagers or adults wanted to become monks or nuns, they first lived in the monastery as novices. Novices were supervised by the novice-master as they learned the rules of the monastery and how to say prayers. After about a year, novices who showed that they could follow the rules of the monastery and still wanted to join, asked permission from the community. If they were accepted, the novices put on the full habit of their order and took vows of poverty, **chastity**, and obedience.

▲ *When a woman became a nun, her hair was cut, and she was given a habit and wedding ring as a sign that she was married to Jesus Christ. Then, she was blessed by the abbot.*

Running Away

Not all monks and nuns were happy in monasteries, either because they had joined only to please their families or because they did not want to follow the monastery's rules. Some rebelled by breaking the rules. They stole extra food, mumbled their prayers, slept in church, and did not do their work well. Other monks and nuns ran away. Those who were caught were returned to the monastery and punished. Punishments included fasting, having to perform more prayers, being beaten, or being locked in a room.

Orders

Many different groups, or orders, of Christian monks and nuns were formed during the Middle Ages. Some orders were just for men or for women, but some orders welcomed both. Each order had its own set of rules and its own style and color of habit.

Benedictines

During the Middle Ages, the Benedictine Order was the most common order of monks and nuns in western Europe. It was founded by Saint Benedict of Nursia, in Italy, in the 500s. Saint Benedict wanted monks and nuns to do God's work through prayer and work around the monastery. He had them take vows of poverty, chastity, obedience, and stability, which meant that they were expected to remain at the same monastery their whole lives. Many Benedictine monasteries grew wealthy, partly because nobles gave them land and other gifts.

▶ *Benedictine monks wore habits made from black wool, so they were nicknamed "Black Monks."*

Cistercians

The Cistercian Order was founded in 1098 in France by an abbot named Robert of Molesme. The Cistercian Order followed the Benedictine Rule in a very strict way. Cistercians believed that older Benedictine monasteries had become too wealthy and no longer followed the Rule properly. Cistercians believed that returning to a simple life of poverty, prayer, and hard work was the best way to serve God.

◀ *Cistercians were nicknamed "White Monks" because their robes were made of plain, white wool.*

Military Orders

Military orders were groups of monks who were also knights. They protected Christian holy places in the **Middle East** and fought against people whom they considered enemies of Christianity. The Order of the Knights Templar was one of the most famous military orders. It was founded around 1118 to protect Christian **pilgrims** traveling to the holy city of Jerusalem. The Templars also fought for control of Jerusalem and the surrounding countryside during the **crusades**.

◀ *The Templars wore white surcoats with red crosses over their armor.*

Friars

In the early 1200s, new kinds of religious orders appeared. Their members were called friars, which comes from a Latin word meaning "brothers." Unlike monks, who had to stay inside their monasteries, friars usually lived in towns and went out among the townspeople to hear their confessions, **preach**, and visit the sick and dying. Friars were very well educated and many taught at universities.

The best known orders of friars were the Franciscans and Dominicans. The Franciscans were founded by Saint Francis of Assisi in Italy around 1209. Saint Francis and his followers were concerned with leading a simple life, preaching, and helping others. The Dominicans were founded by Saint Dominic in France in 1216. St. Dominic's aim was to fight heresy, or ideas that went against Catholic teaching, through preaching.

▲ *Monasteries were founded for Franciscan and Dominican nuns. Here, Saint Francis is cutting the hair of Saint Clare of Assisi, who established a group of Franciscan nuns known as the Poor Clares in 1212.*

Monks and Nuns in Other Countries

Religions other than Christianity had their own kinds of monks and nuns. They wore distinctive clothing and valued a strict life of chastity, non-violence, and living without personal possessions. In addition, monks in many lands were respected for their learning and were believed to have special powers to help other people.

Hindu Holy Men

Hinduism is the most ancient religion of India. Hindus pray to many gods and goddesses, and believe that the souls of all living creatures are reborn in new bodies after they die. Some Hindus lived apart from others in communities of **hermits** called *ashrams* or in monasteries called *mathas*. They led very strict religious lives in the hope that their next lives would be better. Some Hindu monks practiced exercises called yoga that taught them how to control their breathing and thinking so they could focus on religious thoughts.

▼ *Hindu holy men gave people blessings and advice. They were often given gifts, such as food, in exchange for their help.*

Buddhist Monks

Buddhism is a religion that began in ancient India and spread to China, Japan, and Southeast Asia. Buddhists follow the teachings of a prince named Siddhartha Gautama, who gave up his wealth and left home to live as a monk. Gautama became known as "the Buddha," which means "the **Enlightened** One." Medieval Buddhist monks and nuns followed a set of written rules called the Vinaya. They promised to live in poverty, not to kill, steal, or lie, and not to marry. Buddhist monks spent their days studying, **meditating**, praying, and doing chores in the monastery.

▲ *Buddhist monks and nuns shaved their heads and wore yellow or brown robes.*

Jains

Jainism is an ancient religion in India that is related to Hinduism and Buddhism. In the Middle Ages, Jain monks and nuns took five vows: to not harm any living creature, to speak only the truth, to not take anything that was not given to them, to own nothing, and not to marry. Instead of living in monasteries, they wandered between villages, teaching people their religious beliefs, and praying and performing religious ceremonies in Jain temples.

▶ *Jain monks and nuns covered their mouths with cloth masks to avoid accidentally breathing in and harming insects.*

Eastern Orthodox Monks

Greek Orthodox monks spread Christianity to eastern Europe and the African kingdom of Ethiopia. The Greek Orthodox Church was a part of the Eastern Orthodox Church, but centered in Greece. Orthodox monks and nuns followed daily routines similar to those of Catholic monks and nuns, but they had different rules and customs. Monks wore black habits and cylindrical hats called *skadions*.

◀ *Some Eastern Orthodox monks and nuns painted icons, which are images of Jesus Christ or Christian saints painted on wood.*

Famous Medieval Monks and Nuns

During the Middle Ages, most monks and nuns lived quiet lives in monasteries, but some became famous because of their great learning and teaching. After their death, monks and nuns who had led extremely holy lives were named saints by the Church.

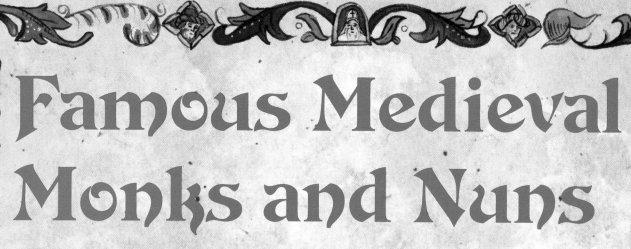

Saint Radegund (520–587) ▶

Radegund was a German princess who was captured in war by the Frankish king Clotar I, from present-day France. Radegund married Clotar I and became queen of the Franks. When the king murdered her brother, Radegund left her husband to become a nun. She founded a monastery in France for 200 noblewomen. Her monastery became famous for study, and attracted scholars and writers from France and Italy.

◀Saint Bernard of Clairvaux (1090–1153)

Bernard was the son of a French knight. After his mother died, he gave up his study of literature and poetry and became a Cistercian monk. In 1117, he was made abbot of a new monastery in Clairvaux and served there for 38 years. Bernard also founded new monasteries for those who wanted to follow him. He became so well known that knights, rulers, and Church leaders, including the Pope, asked him for advice. He wrote the Rule for the Knights Templar and became famous for encouraging Christian knights to join the crusades.

Hildegard of Bingen (1098–1179)

Hildegard was born in present-day Germany. At the age of ten, her noble parents sent her to live with an **anchoress** in a cell attached to a Benedictine monastery. Around 1147, she founded her own monastery of noble Benedictine nuns. Hildegard experienced **visions**, believing them to be messages from God about Heaven and how to be a better Christian. She wrote books about her visions, nature, and medicine. Hildegard was also a poet, artist, and composer of religious music, which is still performed in churches and concert halls today.

Sergius of Radonezh (1314–1392) ▶

Sergius was a Russian Orthodox monk who left the monastery to live as a hermit in the forest. The Russian Orthodox Church was part of the Eastern Orthodox Church, but located in Russia. He believed that by laboring, praying, reading the Bible, and living with animals in nature, he would become a better monk. Sergius attracted other hermits and formed a monastery with them. He gained the nickname "the Builder of Russia" because Russians believed that his prayers helped them defeat the Mongols, a non-Christian people from Asia, who ruled over them.

Martin Luther (1483–1546)

Martin Luther was a friar and teacher in Germany at the end of the Middle Ages. He and his followers disagreed with many teachings of the Roman Catholic Church and wanted to reform, or change it. Luther stopped being a friar and wrote about his new ideas. He did not believe that Mass or life in a monastery pleased God. Luther thought that the wealth and power of monasteries and Church leaders distracted them from leading good Christian lives. Luther's movement to change Christianity became known as the Protestant Reformation. As a result of the Protestant Reformation, many German monasteries closed in the 1500s.

The Monastery

Most monasteries had a similar layout, with an inner courtyard called a cloister surrounded by a church and sleeping and living quarters. Larger monasteries had additional buildings, including infirmaries, houses for abbots, servants' houses, barns, and stables.

Monks and some wealthy people were buried in the monastery's cemetery.

In the lavatorium was a trough filled by a fountain of water in which monks or nuns washed their hands and faces before entering the church or refectory.

West of the cloister were store rooms and a hospice for housing guests of the monastery.

Monks walked, studied, rested, talked, and got fresh air and exercise in the cloister.

The scriptorium was in a sunny part of the monastery so scribes had good light for working.

Monks ate together in a large dining room called a refectory.

The latrines, near the dormitory, were toilets that emptied into a pit or sewer.

The warming room had a fire in which the monks warmed themselves in the winter. The only other heated building was the infirmary.

Often, monks called lay brothers worked the monastery's land, growing food.

Monks met in the chapter house for their daily meeting with the abbot.

Monks slept in the dormitory, often situated above the chapter house.

The church was the largest building in the monastery.

Sick monks or nuns were cared for in the infirmary. Sick people from outside the monastery were cared for in the hospice.

Building a Monastery

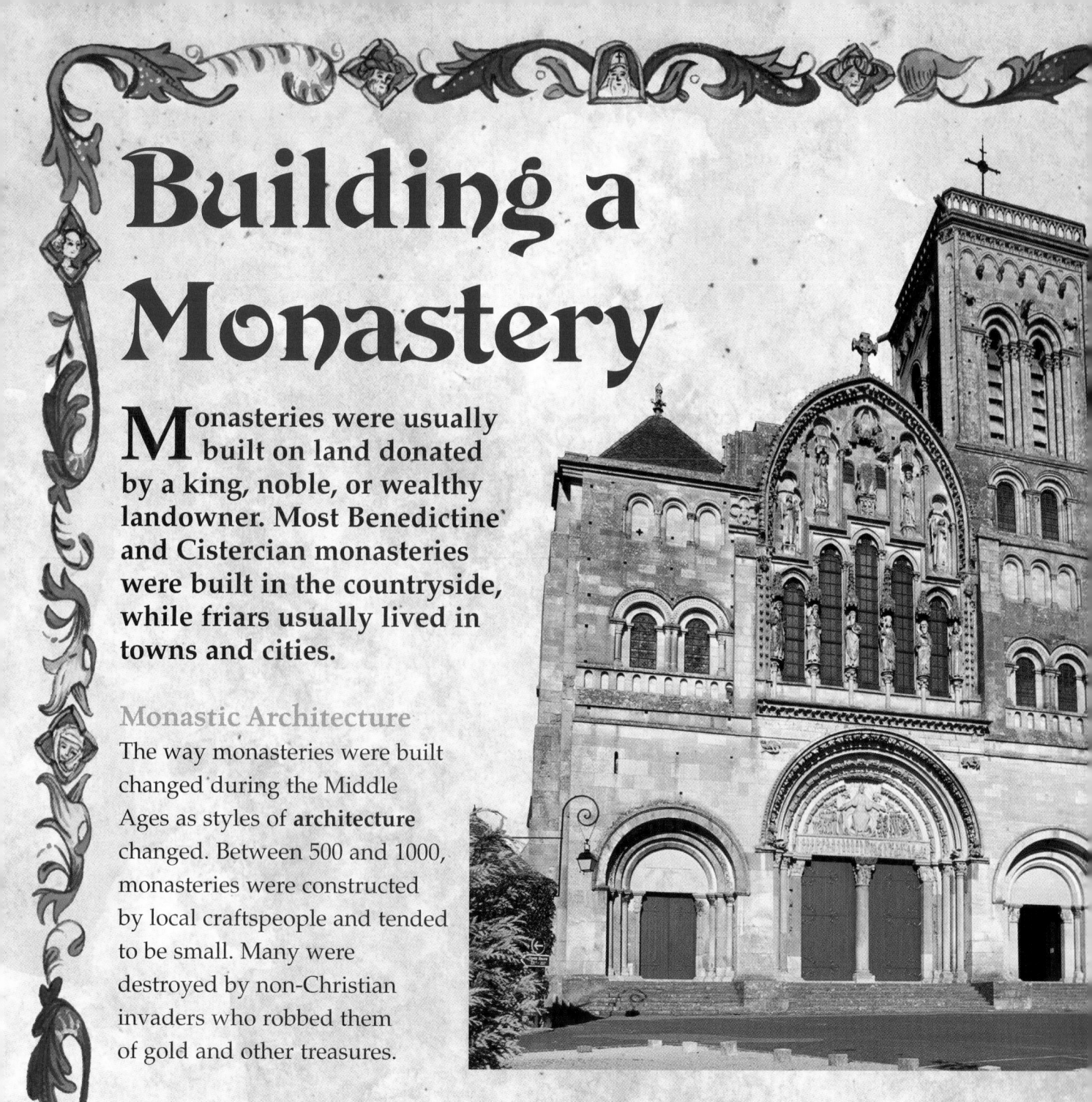

Monasteries were usually built on land donated by a king, noble, or wealthy landowner. Most Benedictine and Cistercian monasteries were built in the countryside, while friars usually lived in towns and cities.

Monastic Architecture

The way monasteries were built changed during the Middle Ages as styles of **architecture** changed. Between 500 and 1000, monasteries were constructed by local craftspeople and tended to be small. Many were destroyed by non-Christian invaders who robbed them of gold and other treasures.

Between 1000 and 1150, the best builders and stone workers from around Europe designed larger churches for monasteries. The churches were designed in the Romanesque style, with thick walls and pillars, and rounded arches. They accommodated the greater numbers of Christian pilgrims visiting saints' tombs or relics.

From 1150 to 1500, monasteries across Europe were built in the Gothic style. The very high stone ceilings of Gothic churches were held up by pointed arches and **buttresses**, so the walls did not have to carry all the weight.

▲ *The church of the Benedictine abbey at Vézelay, France was built in the Romanesque style. The stone ceiling is held up by thick walls, stone columns, and round arches.*

Art in the Monastery

Monasteries were often decorated with sculptures, paintings, and other artwork that illustrated religious stories and reminded people about Christian teachings. Sculptors made carved statues of Jesus and saints from wood or stone. Artists painted beautiful scenes on the walls of churches and refectories. Gold and jewels donated by pilgrims decorated reliquaries, which are boxes that hold the bones or other relics of a saint. The chalices and patens used during Mass were also made from gold and silver and were often decorated with precious jewels. Sometimes, monks or nuns made these treasures, but often craftspeople and artists were hired to make art for monasteries.

▲ *The arched space over a church's entrance often had carved sculptures showing good souls being rewarded by Jesus Christ in Heaven and bad souls being punished in Hell.*

▼ *Gothic churches were decorated with large stained-glass windows that depicted scenes from the Bible. This window shows an angel announcing to Mary that she will give birth to Jesus Christ.*

Famous Monasteries

Some medieval monasteries became famous because the monks or nuns who lived there were great scholars or led very holy lives. Others became known for their beautiful architecture and for the art that decorated them. Monks and nuns still live in some monasteries built in medieval times.

◄ Shaolin Monastery, Honan Province, China

In 496, the ruler of China built a monastery near his capital city for Buddhist monks from India. Shaolin Monastery became an important center for meditation and the study of Buddhist teachings. Over the centuries, Shaolin was destroyed by wars and fires, but was rebuilt many times. It is known for its more than 200 medieval stone pagodas, also called stupas, which are small towers built over graves that honor the memory of the Buddha. Today, Shaolin is famous as the legendary home of kung fu fighting, a form of martial arts.

Monte Cassino, Italy ▶

In 529, Saint Benedict founded his monastery of Monte Cassino high on top of a mountain in Italy. It was destroyed several times during the Middle Ages by wars and earthquakes, but it was rebuilt and remained the most important Benedictine monastery. Monte Cassino was full of art and treasures donated by devoted Christian visitors, and its library contained rare, ancient books that attracted scholars. The monastery was destroyed again during **World War II**, but was beautifully restored and is used today by Benedictine monks.

Saint Catherine's Monastery, Mount Sinai, Egypt ▾

Saint Catherine's Monastery was built between 527 and 565 by the Roman ruler Justinian at the foot of Mount Sinai, Egypt, where Christians believe that God spoke to a prophet named Moses. A high wall around the monastery protected the Greek Orthodox monks who lived there from attacks by bandits. The ceiling of the monastery's church is decorated with mosaics, which are pictures made from thousands of small colored tiles. For centuries, pilgrims journeyed across the Egyptian desert to visit this famous site.

◄ Meteora, Greece

Meteora means "hanging" in Greek, and the monasteries at Meteora, Greece, appear to hang in the air. They were built in the 1300s on top of very high, rocky cliffs for protection against invaders. Supplies and people had to be raised up in baskets tied to ropes. The largest of the monasteries' churches is called the Great Meteoron, built in 1362. It has a domed roof covered with clay tiles, and walls decorated with paintings of Bible stories and saints. Monks still live in Meteora today.

The Abbey of Cluny, France ▾

The Abbey of Cluny was founded in 910 for monks who wished to follow the Benedictine Rule more strictly. Eventually, it became the largest and richest monastery in Europe. The monks who lived there honored God by building a beautifully decorated church in which they spent almost all their time singing prayers and saying Masses. The church, which had carved stone columns and statues, three levels of windows, and colorful wall paintings, was destroyed during the **French Revolution** in the 1790s. A bell tower and smaller clock tower are all that remain of the once-great church.

Glossary

anchoress A woman who lives alone for religious reasons

architecture The art of designing and building structures

buttress An arch that helps support a building or wall

cellaress A woman who takes care of a convent's food and supplies

chastity Purity and goodness in thought and action

cloister The inner courtyard of a monastery

crusades A holy war that Christians fought against Muslims in the 1000s to 1200s to recover the Holy Land, where Jesus Christ lived and died

enlightened To be given knowledge or understanding

French Revolution A fight against the ruling power of France by the people that lasted from 1789 to 1799

Heaven The place where Christians believe God lives and where good souls go after death

Hell The place where Christians believe evil spirits live and where the wicked go after death

hermit A man who lives alone for religious reasons

Latin The language of the ancient Romans and the Roman Catholic Church

meditate To spend time thinking in silence

merchant A person who buys and sells goods

Middle East The region made up of southwestern Asia and northern Africa

modesty Proper behavior and dress

Muslim A follower of Islam. Muslims believe in one God, called *Allah*, and follow the teachings of the prophet Muhammad

philosophy The study of truth, right and wrong, God, and the meaning of life

pigment A colored powder or liquid made from plants and animals, used as coloring

pilgrim A person who makes a religious journey to a holy place

Pope The head of the Roman Catholic Church

preach To give a religious speech, or sermon, in public

prophet A person who delivers a message from God

relic An object, clothing, or body part that once belonged to a holy person

saint A holy person

scholar A learned person

temple A building for worship

tradesperson A worker with special skills to make things, or a person who runs a shop

vision A picture or dream seen in the mind

World War II A war fought by countries around the world from 1939 to 1945

Index

1 2 3 4 5 6 7 8 9 0   Printed in the U.S.A.   0 9 8 7 6 5 4